A Guide for Using

Criss Cross

in the Classroom

Based on the novel written by Lynne Rae Perkins

This guide written by
Melissa Hart, M.F.A.

Teacher Created Resources, Inc.
6421 Industry Way
Westminster, CA 92683
www.teachercreated.com
©2007 Teacher Created Resources, Inc.
Made in U.S.A.
ISBN-13: 978-1-4206-8080-5

Edited by
Heather Douglas
Illustrated by
Kevin McCarthy
Cover Art by
Courtney Barnes

Table of Contents

Introduction 3
Sample Lesson Plans 4
Before Reading the Book 5
About the Author 6
Book Summary 7
Vocabulary Lists 8
Vocabulary Activities 9
Section 1 (*Chapters 1–8*) 10
    Quiz Time
    Hands-on Project: Make a Guitar
    Cooperative Learning Activity: Record a Radio Show
    Curriculum Connections: Geography—Be a Rockhound!
    Into Your Life: Dress for Success

Section 2 (*Chapters 9–15*) 15
    Quiz Time
    Hands-on Project: Class Yearbook
    Cooperative Learning Activity: Beautify Your World
    Curriculum Connections: English—Speaking in Haiku
    Into Your Life: Teach What You Love

Section 3 (*Chapters 16–21*) 20
    Quiz Time
    Hands-on Project: Self-Portrait in Foil
    Cooperative Learning Activity: Adopt an Elderly Friend
    Curriculum Connections: History—Challenges, Then and Now
    Into Your Life: Parents and Children

Section 4 (*Chapters 22–26*) 25
    Quiz Time
    Hands-on Project: Apple Dumplings
    Cooperative Learning Activity: Tourists in Your Own Town
    Curriculum Connections: Health—Diabetes
    Into Your Life: Theory of Life

Section 5 (*Chapters 27–38*) 30
    Quiz Time
    Hands-on Project: Make a Sarong
    Cooperative Learning Activity: Learning and Changing
    Curriculum Connections: Science—Lightning Bugs
    Into Your Life: What I Did Last Summer

After the Book (Post-Reading Activities)
    Any Questions? 35
    Book Report Ideas 36
    Research Ideas 37
Culminating Activities 38
Unit Test Options 43
Bibliography of Related Reading 46
Answer Key 47

Introduction

A good book can enrich our life like a good friend. Fictional characters can inspire us and teach us about the world in which we live. We turn to books for companionship, entertainment, and guidance. A truly beloved book may touch our lives forever.

Great care has been taken with Literature Units to select books that are sure to become your students' good friends!

Teachers who use this unit will find the following features to supplement their own ideas:

- Sample lesson plans
- Pre-reading activities
- A biographical sketch and picture of the author
- A book summary
- Vocabulary lists and suggested vocabulary activities
- Chapter sections including:
  — quiz
  — hands-on project
  — cooperative learning activity
  — cross-curricular connection
  — extension into the reader's life
- Post-reading activities
- Book report ideas
- Research activities
- Culminating activities
- Three different options for unit tests
- Bibliography of related reading
- Answer key

We are certain this unit will be a valuable addition to your own curriculum ideas to supplement *Criss Cross*.

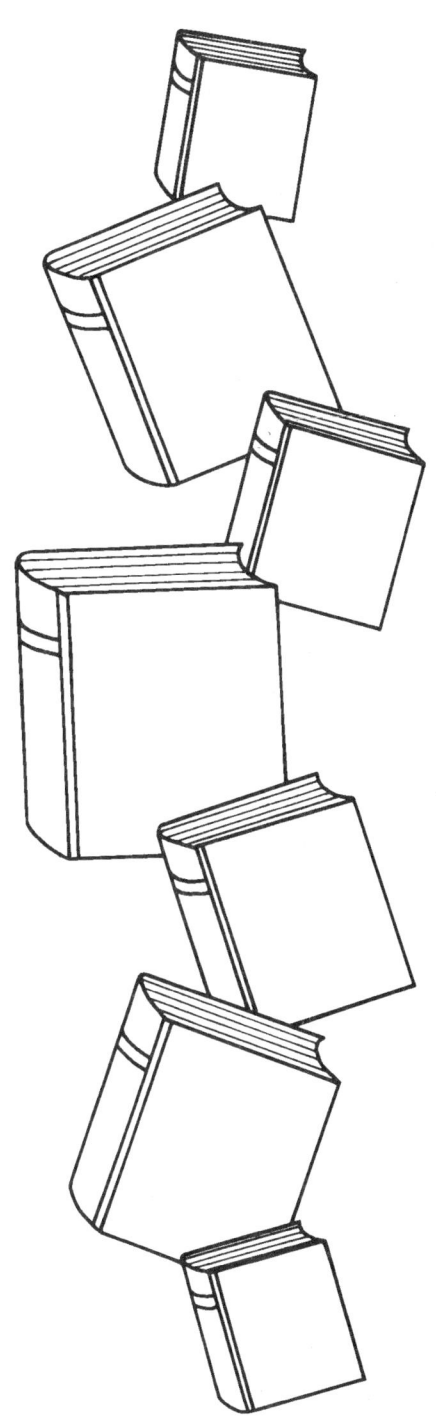

Sample Lesson Plans

The time it takes to complete the suggested lessons below will vary according to the type of activity, your students' abilities, and interest levels.

Lesson 1
- Introduce and complete some or all of the pre-reading activities from "Before Reading the Book." (page 5)
- Read "About the Author" with students. (page 6)
- Introduce the vocabulary list for Section 1. (page 8)

Lesson 2
- Read Chapters 1–5. As you read, discuss vocabulary words, using the book context to explain their meanings.
- Choose vocabulary activities to complete. (page 9)
- Make a guitar. (page 11)
- Record a radio show. (page 12)
- Be a rockhound. (page 13)
- Dress for success. (page 14)
- Administer the Section 1 Quiz. (page 10)
- Introduce the vocabulary list for Section 2. (page 8)

Lesson 3
- Read Chapters 6–9. Discuss vocabulary words.
- Choose a vocabulary activity to complete. (page 9)
- Make a class yearbook. (page 16)
- Beautify your world. (page 17)
- Speak in haiku. (page 18)
- Teach what you love. (page 19)
- Administer the Section 2 Quiz. (page 15)
- Introduce the vocabulary list for Section 3. (page 8)

Lesson 4
- Read Chapters 10–14. Discuss vocabulary words.
- Choose a vocabulary activity to complete. (page 9)
- Make a self-portait in foil. (page 21)
- Adopt an elderly friend. (page 22)
- Learn about challenges in history. (page 23)
- Interview a parent. (page 24)
- Administer the Section 3 Quiz. (page 20)
- Introduce the vocabulary list for Section 4. (page 8)

Lesson 5
- Read Chapters 15–17. Discuss vocabulary words.
- Choose a vocabulary activity to complete. (page 9)
- Make apple dumplings. (page 26)
- Be a tourist in your own town. (page 27)
- Learn about diabetes. (page 28)
- Create a theory of life. (page 29)
- Administer the Section 4 Quiz. (page 25)
- Introduce the vocabulary list for Section 5. (page 8)

Lesson 6
- Read Chapters 18–Epilogue. Discuss vocabulary words.
- Choose a vocabulary activity to complete. (page 9)
- Sew a sarong. (page 31)
- Explore learning and change. (page 32)
- Learn about lightning bugs. (page 33)
- Record your summer. (page 34)
- Administer the Section 5 Quiz. (page 30)

Lesson 7
- Discuss questions students have about the book. (page 35)
- Assign a book report and research activity. (pages 36–37)
- Begin work on one or more culminating activities. (pages 38–42)

Lesson 8
- Choose and administer one or more of the Unit Tests. (pages 43–45)
- Discuss students' feelings about the book.
- Provide the bibliography of related reading. (page 46)

Before Reading the Book

Before you begin reading *Criss Cross* with your students, complete one or more of the following pre-reading activities to stimulate their interest and enhance their comprehension.

1. Examine the cover of the book. Ask students to predict the book's plot, characters, and setting. Ask them if they think the book will be humorous or serious.

2. Discuss the title. Have they heard the phrase "criss cross" used in games or songs before?

3. Answer these questions:
   - Have you ever wished something exciting would happen to you?
   - How do you feel about friendship? Is it important to you?
   - What is your neighborhood like? Can you describe the people in it?
   - How can a special skill or interest enrich your life?
   - Do people in your classroom appear different to you than they did years ago? How?
   - What would you do if someone you liked preferred to be friends with someone else instead?

4. Direct students to work in groups to brainstorm how they might go about helping an elderly person in their neighborhood. Share ideas with the entire class.

5. Direct students to work in groups to list the skills and interests they hope to develop, and ways in which to achieve this. (i.e., lessons, internships, practice, etc.)

6. Brainstorm and list the ways in which a young person can help to change the world for the better. Often, children feel that they have no control. However, simply by offering assistance or sharing a skill such as guitar playing or car repair, young people can make a difference in the world.

7. Work in groups to list ways in which to create a friendly community within your neighborhood. Potlucks, garage sales, lemonade stands, dog-walking assistance, meal delivery for the elderly or sick—all can help build a strong community.

About the Author

Lynne Rae Perkins was born in 1956 and raised in Cheswick, Pennsylvania. Children lived all around her neighborhood, and everyone played in the woods nearby. Lynne Rae loved to read and draw. She decided to become an artist.

After high school, she headed for Pennsylvania State University. She told her adviser that she wanted to illustrate children's books. She earned her Bachelor of Fine Arts degree. Like her character Debbie, she learned to see beauty in unexpected places. She went on to earn her Master's degree at the University of Wisconsin-Milwaukee.

Lynne Rae worked as a graphic designer, and continued to read and draw. Then she met her husband, Bill. Together, they moved to the woods in northern Michigan. They made furniture and grew Christmas trees. Being self-employed, Lynne Rae had a lot of time to draw and paint. She also had two children, Lucy and Frank.

Then, Lynne Rae went to a conference for writers and illustrators of children's book. She showed her artwork to an editor. "Do you write as well?" the editor asked.

"Yes," replied Lynne Rae. She went home and wrote a story to accompany her drawings. Her first picture book, *Home Lovely*, won an honor in the Boston Globe/Horn Book Awards for children's literature. She wrote two more picture books and two novels for young adults.

"I think making books is a way of having conversations with people," says Lynne Rae. "I have been on the reader's side for most of my life. When my first book was reviewed and I realized that a few people besides my mother were actually reading it, I felt lucky to think that I could be on this end of the conversation, too."

Lynne Rae's mother read in a newspaper that *Criss Cross* had a good chance of winning the Newbery Medal. She called her daughter. "It was funny to hear about this from my mother," Lynne Rae says. When she found out that *Criss Cross* had won the Newbery Medal for an outstanding contribution to children's literature, the author was shocked. "I had planned on spending the day walking around my little town with my mouth hung open," says Lynne Rae. "But I have to be in New York to be on 'The Today Show.'"

These days, Lynne Rae lives with her husband and children in Sutton's Bay, Michigan. She has written several other children's books including the companion novel to *All Alone in the Universe*, and four picture books.

Book Summary

Criss Cross
by Lynne Rae Perkins
(Greenwillow, 2005)

Debbie makes a wish that something good would happen to her. In another part of the neighborhood, Hector's sister invites him to a coffeehouse to hear a guitar player. Hector decides that he'll learn to play the guitar. He enrolls in guitar lessons and meets a beautiful girl.

Debbie's neighbor Lenny teaches her to drive his truck. Meanwhile, Hector decides to pick up trash in his favorite ravine and his sister helps him. He begins to get good at playing the guitar and singing.

Debbie develops a crush on Dan Persik, but Dan is interested in another girl. Debbie helps an elderly woman named Mrs. Bruning to take down her laundry. Mrs. Bruning offers her tea, and the two become friends.

Mrs. Bruning's grandson, Peter, comes to visit. He meets Debbie, and the two become friends. Suddenly, Mrs. Bruning falls ill. Debbie knows exactly what to do. She takes Mrs. Bruning to the hospital and offers to help repair the elderly woman's house. Later, Debbie and Peter take an amazing bus trip. Debbie describes the day as "perfect."

Hector goes to the county fair and sees the beautiful girl from guitar class holding hands with Dan Persik. He feels sad, but he begins to feel better when he writes a song.

Peter leaves for California, and he writes Debbie a wonderful letter. The neighborhood organizes a block party. Lenny agrees to roast a pig, and Hector decides to play for the guests at the party. The neighborhood kids end up sitting on the roof, talking about life and love. Hector gives Debbie an unexpected gift, then plays one more song for everyone.

Vocabulary Lists

Below are lists of vocabulary words and idiomatic phrases for each section of chapters. The following page offers ideas for using this vocabulary in classroom activites.

Section 1: Chapters 1–8

loophole	rotisseries
sylph	iridescent
coalesce	regenerate
disembodied	telepathically
humanizing	oblivious
psychically	chivalrous
chasm	primeval
hillbilly	subliminal
materialize	metamorphosis

Section 2: Chapters 9–15

whitewashed	universal
ductwork	stick shift
self-preservation	resuscitate
cavernous	ravine
emote(d)	magnitude
sonorous	metaphor
melancholy	picturesque
derision	savoir faire
monsoon	nonchalant

Section 3: Chapters 16–21

haphazard	sarcastic	poised
heft(ed)	prelude	variegate(d)
involuntarily	delphinium	coronet
Siberian	subgroup	sacrilegious
crone	sanctuary	indignant
falsetto	persimmon	vandal

Section 4: Chapters 22–26

refinement	inspirational	dictator(s)
periodically	claustrophobic	monolithic
animated	insulin	circulatory
mute(d)	diabetic	discombobulated
guffaw(s)	tympani	belligerent
ally	depose	ornery

Section 5: Chapters 27–38

steppes	luau	moron
offhandedly	sarong	disoriented
undercurrent	resilient	drone
inadvertent(ly)	conga	disheveled
nebula(e)	bizarre	inaudible
vaulting	cubicle	exasperated

Vocabulary Activities

You can help your students learn the vocabulary words in *Criss Cross* by providing them with the stimulating vocabulary activities below.

1. Ask students to work in groups to create an **Illustrated Book** of the vocabulary words and their meanings.

2. Group students. Direct groups to use vocabulary words to create **Crossword Puzzles** and **Word Searches**. Groups can trade puzzles with each other and complete, then check each other's work.

3. Play **Guess the Definition**. One student writes down the correct definition of the vocabulary word. The others write down false definitions, close enough to the original definition that their classmates might be fooled. Read all definitions, and then challenge students to guess the correct one. The students whose definitions mislead their classmates get a point for each student fooled.

4. Use a word in five different sentences. Compare sentences and discuss.

5. Write a **Short Story** using as many of the words as possible. Students may then read their stories in groups.

6. Encourage your students to use each new vocabulary word in a conversation five times during one day. They can take notes on how and when the word was used, and then share their experience with the class.

7. Play **Vocabulary Charades**. Each student or group of students gets a word to act out. Other students must guess the word.

8. Play **Vocabulary Pictures**. Each student or group of students must draw a picture representing a word on the chalkboard or on paper. Other students must guess the word.

9. Challenge students to a **Vocabulary Bee**. In groups or separately, students must spell the word correctly, and give its proper definition.

10. Talk about **Parts of Speech** by discussing the different forms that a word may take. For instance, some words may function as nouns, as well as verbs. The word "drone" is a good example of a word which can be both a noun and a verb. Some words that look alike may have different meanings; in *Criss Cross*, the word "poised" is used to describe someone who is confident and dignified, but it may also be used to describe an object which is perfectly balanced.

11. Ask your students to make **Flash Cards** with the word printed on one side and the definition printed on the other. Have students to work with a younger class to help them learn the definitions of the new words, using the flash cards.

12. Create **Word Art** by writing the words with glue on stiff paper, and then cover the glue with glitter or sand. Alternatively, students may write the words with a squeeze bottle full of jam on bread to create an edible lesson!

Section 1: Chapters 1–8 · Criss Cross

Quiz Time

Answer the following questions about Chapters 1–8.

1. What does Debbie wish for? _____

2. What does Hector notice about the musician at the coffee house? _____

3. Why does Rowanne take Hector to the coffee house? _____

4. How long have Debbie, Phil, and Lenny known each other? _____

5. Why do Hector and Phil offer their seats in the truck to Debbie and Patty? __

6. Why do Debbie and Patty change their clothes in a rhododendron bush? ___

7. What are Lenny's particular talents? _____

8. What does Debbie discover about the basin-wrench tool? _____

Section 1: Chapters 1–8

Make a Guitar

Hector finds himself enchanted by the guitar player at a coffeehouse. He decides to learn to play the guitar. You can make your own guitar with just a few simple materials.

Materials

- a shoebox or other sturdy box with a fitted lid
- ruler
- pencil
- scissors
- 5–6 rubber bands, in a variety of sizes
- paint, crayons, markers, glitter, sequins, streamers, and other decosrations

Directions

1. First, trace a circle 4" in diameter in the middle of the lid of your sturdy box. Use the scissors to cut out a hole.

2. Now, decorate your guitar. If Hector had made a guitar, he might have decorated it with butterflies, or with pictures of dogs. How can you create your guitar so that it reflects your individuality—that is, who you are as a person?

3. Finally, stretch the rubber bands around the box and arrange them across the hole you cut out. Try to arrange thinner, tighter rubber bands near the top of the hole, and wider, looser rubber bands near the bottom. When you pluck the rubber bands, they produce sound waves. Note which rubber bands create higher-pitched sound waves, and which create lower-pitched sound waves.

4. Now that you have finished your guitar, practice playing it. You might consider getting together with a few other students and composing a song in a group. Perhaps you'll give a solo performance, or arrange a composition that your entire class can play!

Record a Radio Show

Almost every Saturday, Lenny, Hector, Phil, Debbie, and Patty listen to a radio show in a pickup truck. The show is called "Criss Cross."

You can hear radio shows on various subjects on your local station, or online. Among the most popular are "This American Life" (www.thislife.org), "Car Talk" (www.cartalk.com) and "Says You" (http://www.wgbh.org/radio/saysyou/).

Listen to a few, and then plan and record your own 10–15 minute radio show according to the guidelines below:

1. Form groups of four. Talk about what type of radio show you will produce and record. You might want it to focus on advice for pet owners. Maybe you want to focus on events that happen at your school. Or perhaps your radio show, like "Criss Cross," will feature funny songs and jokes.

2. Now, decide how you will record your radio show. Will you record it using a tape recorder, or will you record it as a digital file on your computer, using a microphone?

3. Fill out the informational sheet below and present it to your teacher:

   A. Names of people in the group: _____

   B. Title of our radio show: _____

   C. Brief description of our radio show: _____
   _____

   D. Write out a script of your show, including any interviews or music you might include, and present it to your teacher along with this informational sheet.

4. Finally, record your radio show. Listen to it and make changes as needed. Then, pop popcorn and play your radio show for your class!

Section 1: Chapters 1–8

Be a Rockhound!

Rockhounds are people who enjoy collecting and identifying rocks. Lenny spends hours identifying the rocks in his driveway. What rocks make up the ground around your school or home? Why not document the geology of your location with illustrations and photographs, as Lynne Rae Perkins has done in *Criss Cross*? Then, you too can be a rockhound!

Materials

- magnifying glass
- rock identification book, encyclopedia, or website
- sketchbook or blank paper on clipboard
- pencil
- colored pencils (optional)

Directions

1. First, check out a rock identification book from your local library, or refer to classroom encyclopedias or websites.

2. Then, map out a few square feet of ground that you would like to study. Choose a rock that interests you and examine it through a magnifying glass. Notice the following characteristics about your rock:

color	hardness or softness
shape	texture
size	weight

3. Make a sketch of your rock in your sketchbook or on a blank piece of paper. You may choose to use colored pencils to enhance your sketch.

4. Now, identify the type of rock using your book, encyclopedia or website. Label the type of rock you've found, just as Lynne Rae Perkins labels quartzite and sandstone in her illustration in *Criss Cross*.

5. Try to identify and sketch at least four different types of rocks. Then, post your findings on a bulletin board and compare your discoveries with those of other students. What types of rocks are most common in your area? Which are the least common? Which rock is your favorite, and why?

For additional information on becoming a rockhound, type the keywords "rocks," "kids," and "geology" into your favorite search engine!

Section 1: Chapters 1–8

Criss Cross

Into Your Life: Dress for Success

Debbie and Patty change their clothes in a rhododendron bush. Debbie reflects on how, even though the plaid bell-bottoms her mother suggests are all wrong, she says that she likes them. Later, she rips out the hem in her jeans so that they will drag on the ground. She believes that "wearing the dragging jeans did not actually guarantee that good things would happen to you, but not wearing them could almost guarantee that the good things wouldn't."

Think about your favorite article of clothing. Write a vivid description in the space below to describe the clothing. Make sure to describe color, size, shape, material, the way the item makes you feel when you're wearing it, and why you like it so much.

_____
_____
_____
_____
_____

Now, describe one good thing that happened to you while wearing your favorite article of clothing. Do you think that wearing this particular item helped the good thing to occur?

_____
_____
_____
_____

Sketch your favorite article of clothing below. Then, share your descriptions with your classmates.

#8080 *Criss Cross*   14   ©*Teacher Created Resources, Inc.*

Section 2: Chapters 9–15   Criss Cross

Quiz Time

Answer the following questions about Chapters 9–15.

1. Why does Hector agree to take free guitar lessons from the Presbyterian youth minister?

   _____

   _____

2. Who shares a conversation in the dark in Chapter 10? _____

   _____

3. Why does Debbie wish that there were other kids besides her and Lenny in the truck?

   _____

4. What secret do Lenny and Debbie share? _____

   _____

5. Why does Hector pick up garbage from the ravine? _____

   _____

6. Where does Rowanne think Hector should take a girl? _____

   _____

7. Why does Debbie feel like she doesn't know how to be her own age? _____

   _____

8. What does Hector realize about playing the guitar? _____

   _____

Class Yearbook

Debbie and Patty sit in a wooden gazebo and look at their new school yearbooks. Yearbooks feature photos of students, sometimes with quotes below the pictures to describe each student.

You can create a classroom yearbook in which each student is responsible for one page describing him/herself.

Note to Teacher

After each student creates a yearbook page, place pages in a photo album or scrapbook for a class yearbook. If you'd like each student to have his or her own yearbook, photocopy each page and place them in three-ring binders.

Materials

- photo album or scrapbook with removable pages, one for each student
- pens, markers, glitter, sequins, magazine pictures, colored paper, and other decorations
- scissors
- glue and/or paste
- one photo of each student
- three-ring binders (optional)

Directions

1. First, think about your yearbook page and how you will design it. How can you use decorations, art, and text to best represent your personality?

2. Glue your photo onto the page and decorate the page with illustrations. You might choose to create a collage. You might want to use more than one photo. You are free to be as creative as you'd like with this page—it's all about you!

3. Include one quote that best describes you and write it somewhere on your page. The words can be your own, or they can be from someone famous.

4. Let your page dry if you've glued objects onto it. Then, add it to your classmates' pages to make a yearbook.

5. Display your book at your annual Open House or at a class party.

Beautify Your World

Hector notices that the ravine is a lovely place once it is free of trash. There are beautiful bushes and small furry animals. You can beautify your school or yard by planting a small garden that attracts birds and butterflies.

Materials

- 4 untreated wooden planks, 4' x 1' x 1"
- 8 woodscrews
- cordless drill
- 1 cubic foot of compost
- 1 cubic foot of planting soil
- 1 cubic foot of vermiculite
- 1 cubic foot of peat moss
- shovel
- extra dirt if needed
- packets of seeds for planting
- 6–8 craft sticks
- glue

Directions

1. First, create a garden box out of planks. Screw the planks together into a square and place the box in a sunny location outside.

2. Now, fill your garden box with compost, planting soil, vermiculite, and peat moss. Stir it with your shovel until it is well mixed. If you find that you need more dirt, you can supplement your mixture with more compost and planting soil.

3. Now, plant seeds according to the directions on each package. Radish, pole bean, pea and corn seeds sprout quickly and easily. You might want to plant butterfly and bird-attracting flowers such as marigolds, cosmos, and sunflowers, as well. Mark the area in which you planted each type of seed with the seed packet glued to a craft stick. Make sure to water your garden regularly. Spray it gently so that you don't disturb the seeds. Keep the soil moist until seeds sprout. Later, when your plants are several inches high, you can water more heavily.

   If you enjoy your 4 x 4 foot garden, consider adding another! Books like *The Square Foot Garden* can teach you how to grow numerous vegetables and flowers in small spaces. Type the words "gardening" and "kids" into your favorite search engine for more information on how to beautify your world!

Section 2: Chapters 9–15

Criss Cross

Speaking in Haiku

Haiku is a form of ancient Japanese poetry. Traditionally, a haiku is three lines long and explores some aspect of nature. The first line contains five syllables, the second line contains seven syllables, and the final line contains five syllables.

Here is a famous haiku by the poet Basho:

The old pond is still.
A frog leaps right into it
splashing the water.

Debbie and Patty sit in a Japanese gazebo and talk. Eventually, their conversation turns into haiku. Although they speak about other kids in their class, they stick to the traditional 5–7–5 syllable pattern.

Below, create a conversation between two people who speak in haiku, just as Lynne Rae Perkins does in *Criss Cross*.

Make sure that your haiku reflects the traditional three-line, 5–7–5 syllable format!

#8080 Criss Cross 18 ©Teacher Created Resources, Inc.

Section 2: Chapters 9–15

Teaching What You Love

Lenny teaches Debbie to drive a truck. He shows her how to push the clutch and gas pedals, and how to put the truck into gear. He loves driving, and after he teaches Debbie, she loves driving, too!

What do you love to do? How can you teach someone else, so that they feel the same joy and excitement? Answer the questions below, and then follow the instructions.

1. What do you love to do? List one example here:

   _____
   _____

2. Decide how you can best teach this skill. Then, write out an instruction booklet, plan a demonstration of the skill, or develop a hands-on lesson plan that will allow people to try this skill themselves.

3. Using complete sentences, describe the steps needed to learn this skill:

   _____
   _____
   _____

Now that you have identified something that you love to do and how to teach it, consider giving a five-minute presentation to your class. Here are some possibilities:

*If you love to make sushi, consider bringing the ingredients to class and showing students how to prepare and roll sushi. Give everyone a sample to taste!

*Perhaps you love to play the drums. Bring your set to class one day and teach your classmates how to play a simple drum solo. You might want to demonstrate one of your own compositions, as well.

*Maybe you love to tap dance. Why not demonstrate your skill to music, and then teach your fellow students a short routine? The day before your lesson, remind everyone to wear hard-soled shoes so that they can hear themselves tap!

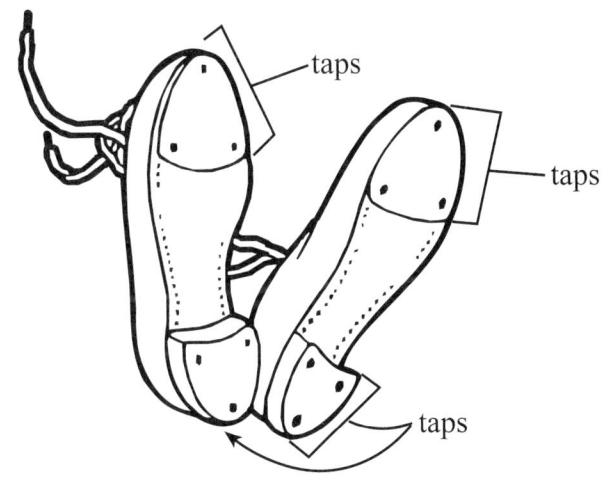

Section 3: Chapters 16–21   Criss Cross

Quiz Time

Answer the following questions about Chapters 16–21.

1. What lessons does Dan Persik need to learn? _____
   _____
   _____

2. Why does Hector sing "Totally Fine" in so many different ways? _____
   _____
   _____

3. Why does Dan put Debbie's necklace in his pocket? _____
   _____
   _____

4. Why does Debbie like to listen to her mother's stories about her? _____
   _____
   _____

5. How do Debbie and Mrs. Bruning become friends? _____
   _____
   _____

6. Why does Mrs. Bruning tell Debbie that she's "free at last"? _____
   _____
   _____

7. Why do the statues of the saints have boxes over them at Phil's church? _____
   _____
   _____

8. How do the kids get Lenny's father's truck to start? _____
   _____
   _____

Section 3: Chapters 16–21   Criss Cross

Self-Portrait in Foil

While looking through her mother's box, Debbie finds a booklet on creative ways to use aluminum foil. You can make an artistic self-portrait out of aluminum foil to hang on the wall.

Materials

- poster board
- paper towels
- glue
- scissors
- shoe polish
- corrugated cardboard, one 8½" x 11" piece for each student
- pencils (not too sharp)
- heavy-duty aluminum foil
- lace, doilies, textured wallpaper, string (optional)

Directions

Draw and cut shapes from poster board to symbolize you and your interests. Trace each shape on a paper towel and cut the towel to fit. Glue the towel onto the poster board shape. Then, glue your shapes, towel-side up, to your piece of corrugated cardboard. Let dry.

Now, cover your cardboard with a piece of aluminum foil, and fold edges 1" over the back. Secure with glue. Use a dull pencil to etch patterns and words into the foil. Glue lace, string, doilies, and other textured objects onto the foil to add interest.

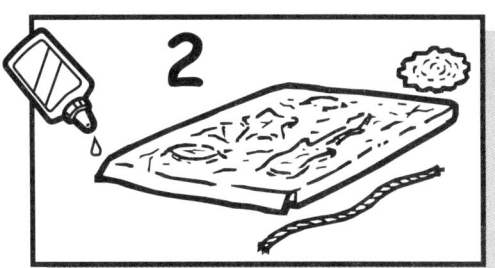

Finally, cover your foil with a thin layer of shoe polish. Allow the polish to dry. Hang your foil self-portrait on a bulletin board for others to enjoy.

Section 3: Chapters 16–21

Criss Cross

Adopt an Elderly Friend

Debbie finds many rewards in helping Mrs. Bruning with her laundry, cleaning, and other tasks. Many elderly people welcome the company of young people. Many have boxes full of fascinating memorabilia, and would love to share their stories of the past.

As a class, you can adopt a local retirement center and befriend the residents. First, contact the center's manager. Write down visiting hours, and find out whether children are welcome to come. Ask the manager to match your class up with a group of elderly residents. Make a date to visit the center.

On visiting day, break into groups of three or four. Each group should visit with one resident at the center for 45 minutes to an hour. Your group might want to ask the following questions of your older friend:

1. What was life like when you were my age?

   _____
   _____

2. What did you do for fun?

   _____
   _____

3. What do you know now that you wish you had known when you were my age?

   _____
   _____

4. Tell me about your family and/or pets.

   _____
   _____

5. What do you like to do for fun now?

   _____
   _____

Write down the answers to these questions. Before you say goodbye to your new friend, consider taking a picture of him or her with your group.

When you return to your classroom, write about your experience in a short report. Present it to the class. Then, make a copy of your report for your elderly friend. Enclose it in a thank you card, handmade by the people in your group.

Consider adopting your new friend for longer than just one day. You may choose to visit now and again, or to send holiday cards or treats. Your friend will thank you!

Section 3: Chapters 16–21   Criss Cross

Challenges, Then and Now

> She had heard about the Depression, polio, and scarlet fever. About her grandfather coming home from work with his white collar gone gray, from all the soot and ash, just in the air, from the steel mills. – *Criss Cross* by Lynne Rae Perkins

As Debbie looks through her mother's pictures and souvenirs, she reflects that the past looks nicer than the present. Then she remembers that the past, like the present, has its share of challenges.

Using books, encyclopedias, and the Internet, do research on the challenges Debbie mentions and fill in the blanks below. Then, research economic, health, and environmental challenges that exist in your world today.

Economic Challenge	
The Depression	**Name an economic challenge that exists today:**
a. Describe it in a sentence.	a. Describe it in a sentence.
b. When did it take place?	b. When does it take place?
c. Who was affected?	c. Who is affected?

Health Challenge	
Polio or Scarlet Fever	**Name a health challenge that exists today:**
a. Describe one or the other in a sentence.	a. Describe it in a sentence.
b. When did it take place?	b. When does it take place?
c. Who was affected?	c. Who is affected?

Environmental Challenge	
Air Pollution from Steel Mills	**Name an environmental challenge that exists today:**
a. Describe it in a sentence.	a. Describe it in a sentence.
b. When did it take place?	b. When does it take place?
c. Who was affected?	c. Who is affected?

©Teacher Created Resources, Inc.   23   #8080 Criss Cross

Parents and Children

Debbie spends a long time looking through her mother's childhood relics. She discovers a lot about her mother—what she collected, movies she saw, clothing she wore. What do you know about the adults in your life? Choose one adult to interview. This might be a parent, an aunt or an uncle, grandmother or grandfather, or a family friend. Answer the following questions for your chosen adult, and then for yourself.

Adult

1. What did you like to collect as a young person?

2. What was your favorite item of clothing when you were my age?

3. What was your favorite movie?

4. What did you consider to be a great challenge when you were growing up?

5. What was your favorite thing to do as a young person?

6. What particular skill were you good at when you were my age?

You

1. What do I like to collect?

2. What is my favorite item of clothing?

3. What is my favorite movie?

4. What is a great challenge for me right now?

5. What is my favorite thing to do?

6. What particular skill am I good at?

Section 4: Chapters 22–26

Criss Cross

Quiz Time

Answer the following questions about Chapters 22–26.

1. Why does Lenny decide to work on his dirt bike in the yard? _____

2. What does Debbie notice about Phil's hands? _____

3. Why does Peter offer to help Grossi around the house? _____

4. Why doesn't Mrs. Bruning's telephone work? _____

5. Why does Debbie drive Mrs. Bruning's car? _____

6. Why does Hector believe himself to be an idiot? _____

7. How does Dan react when Russell speaks to him? _____

8. Why do Debbie and Peter get on a bus? _____

Apple Dumplings

After teasing Hector about the calories in a fried elephant ear, Dan eats an apple dumpling! While not low in fat, apple dumplings are delicious, and apples are very good for you! Make the following recipe and see why Dan loves this treat so much.

Note to Teacher: A week before making this recipe, send out a notice to parents along with a copy of the recipe. Ask them to report any food allergies to you, and request that they send a small treat for substitution if a student is allergic to the following ingredients:

Apple Dumplings

Serves 4–6

Ingredients and Materials

- 2 T. granulated sugar
- 1 t. cinnamon
- 1/3 c. chopped walnuts
- 2 c. all-purpose flour
- 4 t. baking powder
- 1 t. salt
- 4 T. shortening
- 6 medium apples such as Granny Smith, peeled and cored
- medium-sized bowl, small bowl
- sifter
- floured board
- rolling pin
- baking sheet

Directions

1. Preheat your oven to 350º (degrees). Mix together sugar, cinnamon, and walnuts in small bowl. Set aside.

2. In medium bowl, sift together flour, baking powder, and salt. Gently and quickly blend shortening into the mixture with your fingers, until the mixture is crumbly and uniform in size.

3. Put dough on floured board. Divide it into six pieces. With the rolling pin, roll each piece out in a circle until it is large enough to wrap around one apple.

4. Put apple in the center of rolled-out circle. Do not wrap yet! Sprinkle the sugar mixture equally into the core of each apple.

5. Now, wrap the dough around the apple and gather it at the top. Lightly mist or wet the edges to seal dough together.

6. Place each dumpling on a lightly-greased baking sheet. Bake at 350º (degrees) about ½ hour, until apples are tender and the dough is crispy.

    You may choose to serve your apple dumplings with vanilla ice cream, frozen yogurt, whipped cream, or refrigerated vanilla yogurt. Enjoy!

Section 4: Chapters 22–26

Tourists in Your Own Town

Thanks to Peter, Debbie begins to see her hometown in a new way. From the city bus, Seldem looks even more different. You can pretend to be a tourist in your home town. Notice unusual stores, people, and landmarks by participating in the following activity.

Materials

- notebook and pen or pencil
- audio recorder (optional)
- video recorder and laptop computer (optional)
- camera (optional)
- wristwatch or other timekeeping device

Note to Teachers

You may want to assign each student group an adult chaperone.

Directions

1. Walk with your class to the center of town. If your school is in a rural area, consider taking the city bus or asking parent volunteers to drive.

2. Designate a meet-up spot. Break into groups of four. Decide in which direction each group will walk. (This activity works best if each group takes a different direction.) Each group must have a notebook, pen or pencil, and a wristwatch.

3. Synchronize your wristwatches. Each group has half an hour to walk around town and notice interesting and unusual stores, people, landmarks, buildings, public art, plants, birds, animals, etc. Take notes on what you see. Additionally, you might want to take pictures with a camera, or record audio or video accounts of your tour.

4. At the end of half an hour, return to your meet-up spot. Each group has five minutes to do a short presentation on what members noticed about their particular tour. Consider offering audio, video, and/or picture representations of your section of town.

5. Consider concluding your excursion by sharing a picnic lunch at your meet-up spot, and discuss further exciting aspects of your town!

Section 4: Chapters 22–26

Diabetes

Mrs. Bruning is diabetic. She becomes ill, and Debbie recalls a television program in which someone gives a diabetic a glass of orange juice with sugar. Debbie does this for Mrs. Bruning, and the older woman begins to recover.

A diabetic attack can look frightening; however, a few first aid techniques can improve the victim's health in just minutes.

Using encyclopedias, books, and the Internet, take the Diabetes Quiz below.

1. Diabetes is a/an:
   a. illness that makes you dependent on orange juice
   b. disease that causes sugar to build up in your blood
   c. injury that makes you dizzy and mean
   d. disease that causes your body to make too much insulin

2. Insulin is:
   a. another name for diabetes
   b. found in jelly and jam
   c. not something our body needs
   d. a hormone that transfers glucose into our cells

3. The most common type of diabetes is:
   a. Type 2 diabetes
   b. Type 3 diabetes
   c. Type 1 diabetes
   d. gestational diabetes

4. What is Mrs. Bruning supposed to do with the bottles of insulin in her refrigerator?
   a. drink them four times a day
   b. put them in orange juice
   c. save them for an emergency
   d. regularly inject them into her body

5. What two actions can help reduce the possibility of developing diabetes?
   a. exercise and healthy eating
   b. eating sugary foods and watching TV
   c. resting and drinking soda once a day
   d. gaining weight and playing video games

6. Symptoms of diabetic shock include:
   a. sour breath and too much energy
   b. high blood sugar
   c. sweetish breath and dizziness or fainting
   d. hyperactivity and anger

7. You can help someone in diabetic shock by offering:
   a. a glass of fruit juice
   b. a piece of hard candy
   c. a glucose tablet
   d. any of the above

Section 4: Chapters 22–26 Criss Cross

Theory of Life

Peter impresses Debbie with his theory of life. He believes it's important to leave your usual surroundings to find pieces of yourself that make up your whole being. Debbie's theory is that on this day, she has a perfect place in a perfect world.

The word "theory" relates to philosophy—that is, your beliefs and values. What is your theory of life? What are your beliefs? What is important to you? What does it mean to be alive?

Record your theory in two detailed paragraphs in the space below. Afterward, consider sharing your theory with a small group of classmates, or read your theory out loud in front of your entire class.

Section 5: Chapters 27–38   Criss Cross

Quiz Time

Answer the following questions about Chapters 27–38.

1. Why does Hector feel he has something in common with the stepped-on worms?

   _____

   _____

2. Why does Debbie spend so much time dusting Mrs. Bruning's living room?

   _____

   _____

3. Why does Debbie's mother keep the little figurines of dogs? _____

   _____

   _____

4. What good thing happens to Debbie? _____

   _____

   _____

5. How does Dan treat the man without legs?_____

   _____

   _____

6. Why does Hector put the necklace in his pocket?_____

   _____

   _____

7. Why does Rowanne's coworker, Becky, invent a boyfriend?_____

   _____

   _____

8. How has Hector changed over the summer?_____

   _____

   _____

Make a Sarong

Hector finds a picture of a luau. In it, the guitarist wears a sarong. You can make a sarong in preparation for the class party (see page 38) to celebrate the conclusion of *Criss Cross*.

Materials

- a piece of colorful fabric, 3–4 yards long, 36"–45" wide
- a box of straight pins
- thread to contrast with or match the fabric
- a sewing needle

Directions

First, you'll need to hem the edges of your fabric. Turn the rectangle over so the printed side is face-down. Fold the edge of one end half an inch toward you, then fold over another half inch. Pin the edge in place with straight pins. Now, sew your hem. Try to make even stitches. Fold, pin, and hem the other three sides of your sarong. Now you are ready to tie your sarong around a pair of shorts or a swimsuit.

First, hold the sarong behind you like this:

Second, pull the ends evenly forward around your waist:

Finally, tie the ends around your waist and secure a knot at your hip, like this:

Alternatively, you may choose to wear your sarong like a dress. With the fabric behind you, pull the ends of the sarong forward so that the material lies against your upper back. Then, gather the ends and cross them over your chest like this:

Now, bring the ends over your shoulders, and secure them around your neck in a like this:

Section 5: Chapters 27–38   Criss Cross

Learning and Changing

Authors make a strong effort to show how the characters in their novels change throughout the story. Some authors do this by describing what their characters learn and why their characters do certain things in their stories. Lynne Rae Perkins creates several characters in *Criss Cross*. Over the course of one summer, each character learns different lessons and changes in particular ways.

Break into groups of 3 or 4. Using the chart below, discuss and record what these characters learn and show how he or she changes throughout the story in Criss Cross.

Character	What This Character Learns	How This Character Changes
1. Debbie		
2. Hector		
3. Lenny		
4. Dan		
5. Peter		
6. Mrs. Bruning		

Now, in your group, make up a short story. Discuss what your characters will learn and how they will change. Then, write your story and share it with the class.

_____

_____

_____

_____

_____

_____

_____

Section 5: Chapters 27–38

Lightning Bugs

At the luau in *Criss Cross*, Debbie asks Lenny what makes the lightning bugs light up. "It's a chemical reaction," he says. "In their abdomens." Then, he points out that this is how male lightning bugs find the females.

"Lightning bug" is another name for fireflies. This insect is fascinating! In different parts of the world, lightning bugs drift about at night like little lanterns, looking for mates.

Do you want to know more about lightning bugs? Go to your school or public library and check out books and encyclopedias. Visit websites such as *http://www.backyardnature.net* or *www.wikipedia.org*.

Study the picture of a lightning bug below. Label its parts, and then fill in the blanks in the sentences below the illustration.

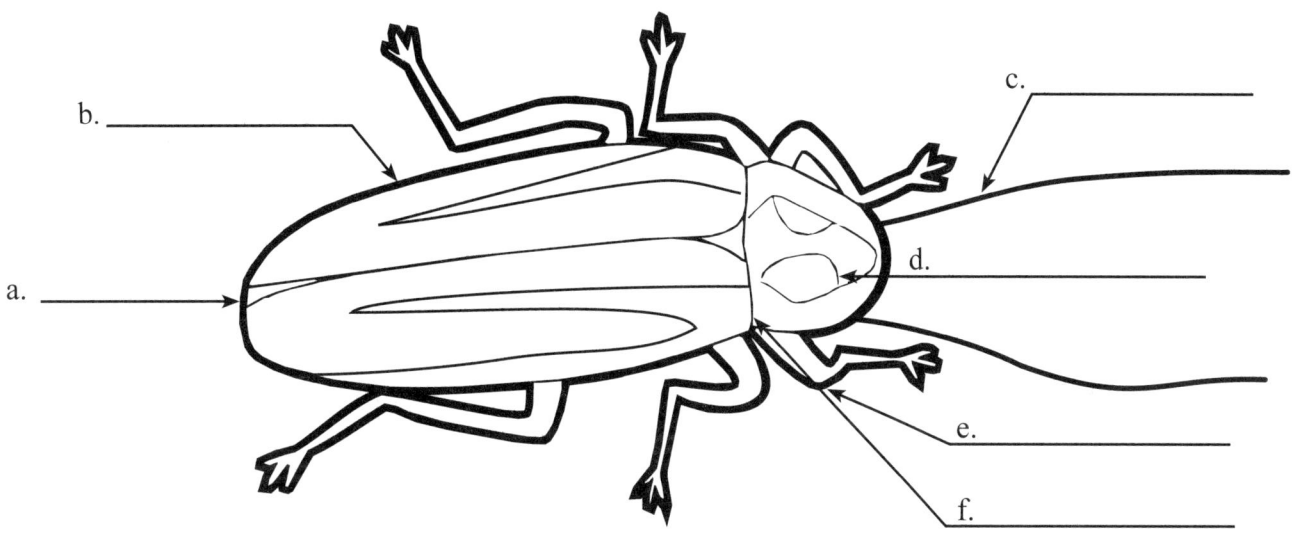

1. Lightning bugs are part of the _____ family.

2. So that lightning bugs don't attract a member of a different species, each species has its own _____.

3. The chemical reaction that causes lightning bugs to glow is also called _____.

4. Larva(e) is another name for lightning bug _____.

5. Lightning bug larvae have mandibles which inject a chemical that _____ their prey and helps to digest it.

Challenge Question: How do female adult lightning bugs practice cannibalism?

_____

_____

What I Did Last Summer

The action in *Criss Cross* takes place over one summer. Summer is a wonderful time of year in which students often don't have to go to school. They have more free time, and the weather is warm. This creates a perfect atmosphere for adventure, as Debbie and Peter discover.

Think about the adventures you had last summer. Did you take a trip, visit family and/or friends, build a treehouse or adopt a dog? What made last summer exciting?

In the space below, write a letter to a good friend. Fill it with vivid details about your summer adventures so that your friend can understand what made the season so special. Include a photo or drawing that best captures your summer experience.

Summer

_____
_____
_____
_____
_____
_____
_____
_____
_____
_____
_____
_____
_____
_____
_____

After the Book   Criss Cross

Any Questions?

When you finished reading *Criss Cross*, did you have any questions that were left unanswered? Write down three of your questions at the bottom of this page.

Work in groups or by yourself to predict possible answers for all or some of the questions you wrote down, as well as those written below. When you have finished, share your predictions with the class.

1. Do Debbie and Peter ever see each other again? _____

2. Does Dan turn out to be a decent person or not? _____

3. What happens with Hector and his guitar-playing? _____

4. Where does Mrs. Bruning end up living? _____

5. Does Debbie tell her mother about Peter? _____

6. What does Lenny decide to do when he grows up? _____

7. Do Debbie and Patty remain friends? _____

8. What happens to Meadow from Hector's guitar class? _____

9. Does Debbie find a boyfriend, and if so, who? _____

10. Does Lenny's father find out that Debbie can drive his truck? _____

11. After Rowanne graduates from college, what does she do? _____

12. Does Debbie's mother ever tell her daughter about the boy who sent her the dog figurines?

    _____

13. What happens to Phil after the summer is over? _____

14. _____

15. _____

16. _____

Book Report Ideas

There are several ways to report about a book after you have read it. When you have finished *Criss Cross*, choose a method of reporting from the list below, or come up with your own idea about how best to report on this book.

Make a Book Jacket

Design a book jacket for this book. On the front, draw a picture that you feel best captures this story. On the back, write a paragraph or two summarizing the main points of this book.

Make a Time Line

On paper, create a time line to show the significant events in the lives of one or two characters. You may illustrate your time line, if you wish.

Design a Scrapbook

Use magazine pictures, photographs, and other illustrations to create a scrapbook that Debbie or another character might keep to document the summer. Debbie might choose to decorate her scrapbook with the photo of Peter, her damaged necklace, pictures of herself and Patty, and Peter's letter. Hector might paste his own song lyrics into his scrapbook, along with a pressed daisy and a ticket from the Seldem Days Festival.

Make a Collage

Using old magazines and photographs, design a collage that illustrates the characters' summer adventures in the novel.

Create a Time Capsule

What items might each character from *Criss Cross* put in a time capsule by which to remember how he/she spent the summer? What particular container might this character use as a time capsule?

Write a Biography

Do research to find out about the life of author Lynne Rae Perkins. You may use the Internet (Lynne has her own website at *http://www.lynneraeperkins.com*) or magazines. Write a biography, showing how Lynne's own experiences as a child might have influenced *Criss Cross*.

Act Out a Play

With one or two other students, write a play featuring some of the characters in this novel. Then act out your play for your class.

Make Puppets

Using a variety of materials, design puppets to represent one or all of the characters in *Criss Cross*. You may decide to work with other students to write and perform a puppet show.

After the Book

Criss Cross

Research Ideas

As you read *Criss Cross*, you discovered geographical locations, events, and people about which/whom you might wish to know more. To increase your understanding of the characters, places, and events in this novel, do research to find additional information.

Work alone or in groups to discover more about one or several of the items listed below. You may use books, magazines, encyclopedias, and the Internet for your research. Afterwards, share your findings with the class.

- America in the 1960s
- bell-bottom jeans
- basic guitar chords
- fireflies
- haiku
- yearbook production
- Hawaiian luaus
- roasting a pig
- auto repair
- how to drive
- diabetes diagnosis and treatment
- famous long-distance romances
- the Newbery Award
- *Popular Mechanics* magazine
- *Wuthering Heights*
- basic home repairs
- retirement homes
- church confession
- adopt-a-highway programs
- beach/stream cleanup
- how to sing
- 1960s fashion
- art and the mentally ill
- amputees
- Buddhism
- Siddhartha
- Stonehenge
- Machu Picchu
- local fairs and festivals
- elephant ears
- basic first aid
- dirt bike maintenance and repair

Plan a Luau!

In honor of *Criss Cross*, plan a Hawaiian luau-themed celebration in your classroom. Consider inviting guests—another class, or your family members, to join your party.

Luau Checklist

Three weeks before the luau . . .

- ❏ Decide when and where the luau will occur.
- ❏ Discuss how to work the Hawaiian theme into your luau. Will you wear the sarongs you created from page 31? Will you play your guitars from page 11, and/or broadcast your radio shows from page 12? If you recorded audio or video impressions of your hometown from page 27, you might want to play these at the luau, as well.
- ❏ Decide whether your class wants to invite guests to the luau. You might want to invite parents or a neighboring class to enjoy the festivities. Maybe you'd like to invite your elderly friends from the retirement home you adopted. If so, make and send the invitations on the following page. Consider asking your guests to dress in Hawaiian-themed clothing, as well.
- ❏ Discuss decorations. You might want to display your class yearbook from page 16, photos of your beautification project from page 17, and/or your foil self-portraits from page 21. Think also about how you can create trees and animals specific to Hawaiian luaus in your classroom.

Two weeks before the luau . . .

- ❏ Decide what food and drink you will make as a class. This book provides a recipe for apple dumplings on page 26, and macaroni salad and coconut pudding on page 40. Debbie and Peter would likely enjoy chocolate milk and fresh, warm bread. Lenny would enjoy roast pig. All of the characters would certainly enjoy ice cream cones. What would you and your classmates enjoy eating and drinking at your party?
- ❏ Pass around a sign-up sheet. Each student can bring something unique to the party. Consider bringing traditional Hawaiian food or a potted orchid, or show off a skill such as baton twirling, playing the guitar, or doing a Hawaiian hula dance.
- ❏ Send home a note to students' parents to let them know the day/date of the luau, as well as what the student signed up to bring.

One week before the luau . . .

- ❏ Send home a note reminding students of what they have volunteered to bring for the party.
- ❏ Buy and/or make decorations.

The day before the luau . . .

- ❏ Make apple dumplings, macaroni salad, haupia, and other refreshments to be served.

The day of the luau . . .

- ❏ Decorate the party space.
- ❏ Set up a stereo with your radio show, and an audio/video presentation of your tour through your hometown.

  Enjoy!

Plan a Luau! (cont.)

Come to a Luau!

Date: _____

Time: _____

Place: _____

Hosts: _____

Theme: _____

Luau Recipes

You'll often find variations of macaroni salad and haupia (coconut pudding) at Hawaiian luaus. Here are recipes for both.

Macaroni and Potato Salad
(Serves 8–10)

Salad Ingredients
- 4–5 large potatoes
- 1 c. dry macaroni
- 2 chopped carrots
- 2 chopped celery stalks
- 3 chopped sweet pickles
- 1 c. frozen peas
- 2 chopped green onions
- 2 chopped hard-boiled eggs
- salt and pepper

Materials
- 1–2 large pots
- knife for cutting vegetables (or have adult prepare these)
- colander
- large bowl
- small bowl
- wooden spoon

Dressing Ingredients
- 1 and ¼ c. mayonnaise
- ½ c. Italian dressing
- 2 t. sweet or sour pickle juice
- 1 t. prepared mustard
- dash of dill, rosemary and/or parsley (optional)

Directions
Wash and boil potatoes in a pot until they are tender. When they are cool, cut them into cubes. Cook the macaroni in boiling water, and drain in a colander. Mix the ingredients for the dressing in a bowl and set aside.

Now, gently toss the macaroni with the potatoes and the remaining vegetables and hard-boiled eggs. Mix in the dressing and enjoy!

Haupia
(serves 8–10)

Ingredients
- 12 ounces cold coconut milk
- 1 ½ c. water
- ½ c. + 2 T. sugar
- ½ c. + 2 T. cornstarch

Materials
- saucepan
- wooden spoon
- 8" x 8" pan

Directions
Combine all ingredients in a saucepan. Stir slowly over medium heat until thickened. Lower the heat and cook for ten minutes, stirring constantly. Do not let your haupia form lumps or burn. Finally, pour pudding into a pan and chill it in the refrigerator until it is set. Cut it into squares and serve.

Luau Games

You can play the following games at your luau.

Hula Hoop Contest

Materials

- hula hoops
- Hawaiian music

No one knows who invented the hula hoop, but people have played with it for centuries. It gets its name from hula dancing which involves a swiveling of the hips. For your contest, make sure you have several hula hoops. Put on Hawaiian music and offer prizes for those guests who can hula hoop the longest, the fastest, and even the slowest! Some people can hula hoop around their necks and around their arms and legs. Experiment and have fun!

Pin the Coconut on the Palm Tree

Materials

- butcher paper
- construction paper
- paint
- scissors
- paint brushes
- blindfold
- double-stick tape

Create a tall palm tree out of butcher paper and paint it. You might choose to paint a large branch for which people can aim with their coconuts. Now, create 5–6 coconut cut-outs out of brown construction paper and place double-stick tape on the back.

This game is played just like the classic Pin the Tail on the Donkey. Blindfold one person and give him or her a coconut cut-out. Spin the person around gently and see if he or she can "pin" the coconut on the palm tree.

Limbo Dance

Materials

- broom handle
- Hawaiian music

Ask two people to hold the broom handle—the limbo stick—four feet parallel off the ground. Put on Hawaiian music. Each person gets a turn to dance the limbo under the stick, bending backwards so as not to touch the broom handle. Then, ask the people holding it to lower it half a foot. Once again, take turns trying to bend under the stick without touching it. Ask the holders of the stick to lower it half a foot again, and so on. The dancer who can bend backwards the lowest and dance under the stick wins!

Field Trips and Class Visits

Now that your students have finished *Criss Cross*, they may enjoy taking one or more field trips to locations related to the book, or inviting a guest speaker to visit their classroom.

Choose an activity from the list below and locate the appropriate contact person in the phone book or on the Internet. Be sure to call at least two weeks in advance, to give the staff plenty of time to prepare for the event.

Guitar Teacher

Invite a local guitar teacher to visit your class. Arrange for the music department to loan a few guitars. Ask the teacher to show students the basic chords for folk favorites such as Greensleeves.

Trip to a Coffeehouse

Rowanne takes Hector to a local coffeehouse to hear live music. Locate a coffeehouse in your town and inquire about performances. Make sure that the venue serves herbal tea and juice for students whose parents prefer them not to have caffeine. Walk or use public transportation, and plan on spending at least an hour enjoying the coffeehouse ambiance.

Sixties Expert

Criss Cross is set in the 1960s. Invite visitors who grew up in this era to visit your classroom. Ask students to prepare a list of interview questions beforehand. They will likely want to know what kids in the 1960s wore, what music they listened to, what books they read, and how life was different in that era. Alternatively, invite a history or pop culture professor from the local college to visit your class with slides, Powerpoint™ presentations, etc.

Bicycle Mechanics

Lenny is an expert at fixing things, and Debbie is good with a wrench, as well. Call a local bicycle shop or college and ask a bicycle mechanic to visit your class. Ask your students to bring in their bicycles that day, so that the mechanic can teach them how to maintain their bikes with a few simple techniques and tools.

Yearbook Expert

Debbie and Patty look through their junior high school yearbook over the summer. Often, high schools offer a class in yearbook production, with a staff that creates the book over the course of a school year. Call your local high school and invite the yearbook editor to visit your class, along with a staff writer, photographer, and advertising salesperson. Ask the staff to bring along examples of yearbooks for students to look at. Alternatively, take a field trip to the local high school and give students a first-hand look at yearbook production.

Unit Test: Option One — Criss Cross

Objective Test and Essay

Matching: Write the letter of the correct description next to each character.

_____ 1. Debbie   a. He admires a man who has no legs.

_____ 2. Hector   b. She has a box full of dog figurines from her childhood.

_____ 3. Lenny   c. She is the object of Hector's affections.

_____ 4. Phil   d. She is diabetic and has to go to the hospital.

_____ 5. Patty   e. He admires Debbie for her skills and theories.

_____ 6. Peter   f. She changes out of her jumper in the rhododendrons.

_____ 7. Dan   g. She wishes something good would happen to her.

_____ 8. Mrs. Bruning   h. He learns to play the guitar one summer.

_____ 9. Meadow   i. He thinks school is boring, even though he is smart.

_____ 10. Mrs. Pelbry   j. He notices wooden boxes covering the statues of saints.

True or False: Answer true or false in the blanks below.

_____ 1. Hector shows Meadow the ravine he cleaned up.

_____ 2. Peter writes Debbie a letter and encloses his photo.

_____ 3. Dan can be both polite and insensitive.

_____ 4. Debbie and Patty have an argument over a boy.

_____ 5. Phil and Debbie have only known each other a short time.

Short Answer: Write a brief response on separate paper.

1. In what ways does Debbie's wish that something good will happen to her actually come true?
2. What does Hector learn about himself over the summer?
3. Why does Peter agree to stay with his grandmother for a week and help her?
4. What are Dan's strengths, and what are his weaknesses?

Essay: Respond to the following prompt on a separate piece of paper.

The title *Criss Cross* refers to several different ideas in the novel. Discuss the various ways in which the word is used within the book. What does the author point out about relationships and how they "criss cross"?

Unit Test: Option Two   Criss Cross

Responding to Quotes

On separate paper, explain the following quotes from *Criss Cross* as selected by your instructor:

Chapter 2: "So, I'm not mad or anything, I'm glad I went, but why didn't you just tell me you needed me for an excuse not to go out with Chip-Dip?"

Chapter 4: "There's the weird radio show I heard last week," said Lenny. "I think it's the right time for it to come on. Go around and get in."

Chapter 6: "If you think about it," Patty said, "It shouldn't even matter what we wear. People will like us for who we are."

Chapter 9: "Meadow is, like, a word. It's a really nice word, but it's not usually a name."

Chapter 12: "We'll just go back and forth in the driveway," said Lenny. "First and reverse."

Chapter 14: "Look, there goes Hector. I wonder why he's running. His bag is breaking."

Chapter 18: "I can't get my laundry down from the clothesline," said Mrs. Bruning.

Chapter 24: "Let him spend a week here," said his mother. "Then he'll see."

Chapter 25: "Whoa, Hector, better watch it. Those things can make you fat, you know."

Chapter 26: "You could just get on a bus, the first bus that shows up, and get off somewhere. The first stop."

Chapter 29: "You have a letter," she said. "From California."

Chapter 32: "So, what happened to your legs?"

Chapter 35: "I have a gig at a luau," he said. "Actually, it's just a block party, but they're roasting a pig."

Chapter 38: "I'm glad it's not a voodoo necklace, or I would be in really bad shape."

Unit Test: Option Three

Criss Cross

Conversations

Work in groups according to the numbers in parentheses to write or act out the conversations that might have occurred in each of the following situations in *Criss Cross*.

- Debbie and Peter talk on the phone. (2 people)

- Peter's parents tell Mrs. Bruning that she has to move to a retirement home. (3 people)

- Lenny, Phil, and Hector discuss Debbie and Patty. (3 people)

- Debbie's mother talks to her father about the letter from California. (2 people)

- Meadow tells Dan that she doesn't want to date him anymore. (2 people)

- Debbie, Patty, and Lenny go to hear Hector play guitar at a coffeehouse. (3–4 people)

- Patty's and Debbie's mothers discover the clothes in the rhododendron bush and talk to their daughters. (4 people)

- Lenny and his father have a discussion about whether or not Lenny should go to college. (2 people)

- Peter tells his best friend at home about his visit to Seldem. (2 people)

- The man with no legs tells his wife about meeting Dan. (2 people)

- Lenny's father finds out that Lenny and Debbie have been driving his truck. (3 people)

- Debbie asks her mother about the dog figurines. (2 people)

- Mrs. Bruning talks to Peter about Debbie. (2 people)

- Hector and Debbie say goodbye to Rowanne as she leaves for college. (3 people)

- Dan shows up at the luau and laughs at Hector's sarong. Hector's friends defend him. (2–5 people)

Bibliography of Related Reading

Fiction

Birdsall, Jeanne. *The Penderwicks: A Summer Tale of Four Sisters, Two Rabbits, and a Very Interesting Boy.* Knopf, 2005.

Choldenko, Gennifer. *Al Capone Does My Shirts.* Putnam, 2004.

Creech, Sharon. *Walk Two Moons.* HarperTrophy, 1996.

DiCamillo, Kate. *Because of Winn-Dixie.* Candlewick, 2004.

Hale, Shannon. *Princess Academy.* Bloomsbury, 2005.

Hart, Melissa. *The Assault of Laughter.* Windstorm, 2005.

Henkes, Kevin. *Olive's Ocean.* Greenwillow, 2003.

Hiaasen, Carl. *Hoot.* Knopf, 2002.

Lowry, Lois. *The Giver.* Houghton Mifflin, 1993.

Patterson, Katherine. *Bridge to Terabithia.* HarperCollins, 1977.

Perkins, Lynne Rae. *All Alone in the Universe.* HarperTrophy, 2001.

Sachar, Louis. *Holes.* Farrar, Straus and Giroux, 1998.

Sachar, Louis. *Small Steps.* Delacorte, 2006.

Spinelli, Jerry. *Maniac Magee.* Little, Brown, 1999.

Nonfiction

Anderson, Terry. *The Sixties.* Addison-Wesley, 1998.

Bay, William. *Children's Guitar Chord Book.* Mel Bay, 2000.

Betschart-Roemer, Jean. *It's Time to Learn about Diabetes: A Workbook on Diabetes for Children.* Wiley, 1995.

Cohn, Amy. *From Sea to Shining Sea: A Treasury of Folklore and American Folk Songs.* Scholastic, 1993.

Manus, R. and Harnsberger, L.C. *Kids' Guitar Course, Book 1.* Alfred, 2003.

White, Ellen Emerson. *Where Have All the Flowers Gone: The Diary of Molly Mackenzie Flaherty.* Scholastic, 2002.

Web Sites

http://www.ala.org Type "Newbery Award" into search box for a complete list of novels which have won the award.

http://www.lynneraeperkins.com for a list of the author's novels, teacher resources, and biographical information.

http://www.willamettewriters.com/ywwWhazzup.html for information on contests and other opportunities for young writers.

Answer Key

Page 10
1. Debbie wishes for something good to happen to her.
2. Hector notices that the musician is quite skilled, and that the girls really like him.
3. Rowanne takes Hector to the coffee house so that she can have an excuse for not going out with Skip.
4. Debbie, Phil, and Lenny have known each other since they were babies.
5. Hector and Phil offer their seats in the truck to Debbie and Patty because they are being chivalrous.
6. Debbie and Patty change their clothes in a rhododendron bush because they don't want to disappoint their mothers, but they do want to wear clothes that are stylish.
7. Lenny is particularly good at repairing things, and understanding quickly how things such as cars and human bodies work.
8. Debbie develops respect, and even admiration, for the basin wrench tool.

Page 15
1. Hector agrees to take free guitar lessons from the Presbyterian youth minister because his parents buy him a guitar.
2. Debbie and Patty share a conversation in the dark in Chapter 10.
3. Debbie wishes that there were other people besides her and Lenny in the truck because she feels that the silence between them is awkward.
4. Lenny teaches Debbie to drive his father's truck, and they share that secret.
5. Hector picks up garbage from the ravine because he thinks he'd like to show Meadow the area, and he wants it to look beautiful.
6. Rowanne thinks Hector should take a girl to the Tastee-Freez.
7. Debbie feels like she doesn't know how to be her own age because some girls her age are already shaving their legs and dating, while she is unsure about these things for herself.
8. Hector realizes that it's not hard to make one beautiful sound on the guitar.

Page 20
1. Dan Persik needs to learn humility, compassion, respect, and individual thinking.
2. Hector sings "Totally Fine" in so many different ways because he is trying to find his voice and his style.
3. Dan puts Debbie's necklace in his pocket because he wants to tease her.
4. Debbie likes to listen to her mother's stories about her because they are entertaining, and she always sounds good in them.
5. Debbie and Mrs. Bruning become friends when Debbie helps her with her laundry and they share tea and cookies.
6. Mrs. Bruning tells Debbie that she's "free at last" because her hair was very long, and likely difficult to care for.
7. The statues of the saints have boxes over them at Phil's church to keep the saints from seeing people play games of chance at the carnival, which can be construed as a sin.
8. The kids get Lenny's father's truck to start by pushing it, with Debbie at the wheel to put it in gear.

Page 23
The Depression—a dramatic economic slump that began in 1929 and lasted most of the 1930s. Most industrialized nations were affected, but primarily the United States. Farmers, in particular, suffered hardships, but many other men, women, and children were affected, as well.

Polio is a viral paralytic disease. It is an ancient disease that affected many people. Approximately fifty percent of victims were 3–5 years old before Jonas Salk developed a vaccine in 1953.

Scarlet Fever is an infection that results in symptoms such as rashes, fever, fatigue, sore throat, and vomiting. It has been around since at least the 1600s, and affects people of all ages, but particularly children 4–8 years old.

Air Pollution from Steel Mills dirties the air and causes health problems in all who breathe that air. It began with the construction of the first steel mills in the 1800s. People working in steel mills suffer from respiratory diseases, and much research has proven that animals who breathe in the pollution from steel mills pass on genetic defects to offspring.

Page 25
1. Lenny decides to work on his dirt bike in the yard because Debbie is reading in the yard next door.
2. Debbie notices that Phil moves his hands frequently when he talks, like birds.
3. Peter offers to help Grossi around the house because he wants her to be able to stay in her home.
4. Mrs. Bruning's telephone doesn't work because she has forgotten to pay her phone bill.
5. Debbie drives Mrs. Bruning's car because she needs to get her to the hospital.

Answer Key (cont.)

6. Hector believes himself to be an idiot because he throws away his elephant ear when he sees Dan and Meadow.
7. When Russell speaks to him, Dan doesn't answer. He looks at Russell as if he is a rock, and then leaves.
8. Debbie and Peter get on a bus because they want to see how far they have to travel before things get interesting.

Page 28
1. b
2. d
3. a
4. d
5. a
6. c
7. d

Page 30
1. Hector feels he has something in common with the stepped-on worms because Meadow is dating Dan, and he humiliated himself in front of them.
2. Debbie spends so much time dusting Mrs. Bruning's living room because she wants to look at Peter's picture.
3. Debbie's mother keeps the little figurines of dogs because they were given to her by a boy she liked as a younger woman.
4. Debbie receives a letter from Peter, along with his photo.
5. Dan looks at the man without legs and asks him what happened, instead of ignoring him.
6. Hector puts the necklace in his pocket to give to Debbie as a joke.
7. Rowanne's coworker, Becky, makes up a boyfriend because she wants her coworkers to think she's desirable and popular. Possibly, she's lonely.
8. Over the summer, Hector has become leaner, more thoughtful, and more confident. He has become a good guitar player, as well.

Page 32
1. Debbie learns to drive, and she learns that life is interesting. She gains confidence, and she likes herself more by the end of the summer.
2. Hector learns to play the guitar. He grows leaner and more thoughtful, as well as more confident.
3. Lenny quits chewing tobacco. He becomes more interested in fixing things than in school. He also begins to ask girls to the movies.
4. Dan learns to show kindness to people such as the man with no legs, and he gets a girlfriend. However, the author makes a point that he is still on the cusp of change.
5. Peter learns that he is willing to donate a week of his time to help his grandmother. He changes when he meets Debbie—he enjoys traveling with her, and writes her a letter.
6. Mrs. Bruning learns that she can no longer live independently. She becomes more frail and more forgetful.

Page 33
a. abdomen d. eyes
b. wing   e. legs
c. antennae   f. thorax

1. Lightning bugs are part of the beetle family.
2. So that lightning bugs don't attract a member of a different species, each species has its own flash pattern.
3. The chemical reaction that causes lightning bugs to glow is also called bioluminescence.
4. Larvae is another name for lightning bug babies.
5. Lightning bug larvae have mandibles which inject a chemical that paralyzes their prey and helps to digest it.

Challenge Question: Some already-mated female adult lightning bugs emit flash patterns similar to those females of another species. They attract males of that species. When the male lands, the female eats him!

Page 43
Matching
1. g   5. f   8. d
2. h   6. e   9. c
3. i   7. a   10. b
4. j

True or False
1. False   3. True   5. False
2. True   4. False

Short Answer
1. Debbie learns the value of helping an elderly neighbor and meets a boy she likes.
2. Hector learns that he can play guitar, and he learns that even if you're a kind person, the object of your affections won't always like you.
3. Peter genuinely wants to help his grandmother, but he's also interested in getting to know Debbie better.
4. Dan is strong and charismatic, and he is polite to the man with no legs. However, he is also egotistic and insensitive, and he is unkind to some of his classmates.

Essay
Answers will vary. Accept reasonable and well-supported answers.

Page 44
Grade students on comprehension of the story as evidenced by the lengths of answers and depth of responses.

Page 45
Grade students on comprehension of the story, knowledge of the characters, and creativity.